the secret life of
objects

Dawn Raffel

art by Sean Evers

the secret life of
objects

Dawn Raffel

drawings by Sean Evers

Jaded Ibis Press
sustainable literature by digital means™
an imprint of Jaded Ibis Productions USA

© 2012 copyright Dawn Raffel

First edition. All rights reserved.

ISBN: 978-1-937543-03-7

Library of Congress Control Number: 2012936452

Published by Jaded Ibis Press, *sustainable literature by digital means*™ An imprint of Jaded Ibis Productions, LLC, Seattle, Washington USA jadedibisproductions.com

Interior drawings by Sean Evers. Cover art and design by Debra Di Blasi.

For Brendan and Sean

The following chapters were previously published as follows:

"The Tea Set from Japan," "The Prayer Book," "The Bride's Bible," "The Teacup," "The Florsheim Dog," "Tranqil Ease," and "Garnet Earrings" in *Willow Springs*

"The Lady on the Vase," "The Lock," "The Thing with Wings," "My Grandmother's Recipes," and "The Dress" in *The Brooklyn Rail*

"The Rocking Chair," "The Glass Angel," "The Rug," and "The Mirror" in *The Milan Review*

"The Sewing Box" and "Rascal" in *Salt Hill*

"The Mug" in *Unsaid*

"The Cat" in *Moonshot*

"Yosemite and the Range of Light" in *Everyday Genius*

"The Watch" in *The Collagist*

"Medals" (under the title "As-Is") in *Wigleaf*

"The Nesting Bowls" (under the title "Hungary") in *The Lifted Brow* (Australia)

"The Moonstone Ring" in *Numéro Cinq*

Table of Contents

The Secret Life of Objects

The mug came first: a clay-based receptacle for stimulant, for memory, for story, for tonic for aloneness.

Surveying my house I found myself surrounded by surfaces and vessels, by paper and glass, by cloth, wood, clay, paint, and also my late artist mother's renditions of things.

Already the contents are shifting shape. Already I cannot recall a voice, a year, the way the light fell speckled in a room.

Objects are intractable. We own them. We don't.

All memoir is fiction.

We try to fit the pieces together again.

The Mug

Every morning I drink coffee out of a mug that I took from my mother's house. It is a blue mug from the Milwaukee Art Museum where my mother was a docent during the last years of her life. The image is of a Picasso, a bird.

My mother's death was sudden. It was my stepfather who'd been dying, of stomach cancer, and who'd begun home hospice care. My mother, who'd been despondent ("I was supposed to die first," she told me. "This was not supposed to happen."), did not wake up one morning. The house was left in the way a house is left when someone leaves the world mid-thought. Nothing had been sorted or dispensed with or hidden, and after my stepfather died too, it fell to me to see to the house's contents.

My mother had saved everything. This was the good news and also the bad news. Because she had been an artist, her house was filled with dozens upon dozens of sculptures, in clay and in wood, paintings and drawings, in oil, in acrylic, in charcoal, in pencil, of water and trees and women—so many women from so many angles, clothed, nude; their faces, their bodies, the suggestion of the inner life. Roses abounded. Shells, too, the pinkened insides of conches like portals to dreams. My sister and I could not take them all, and I didn't want them to sit in storage for 20 or 30 years until someone else threw them out. I found a taker for everything except the drawings, wisps of thought, which I tossed, reluctantly. My mother's favorite bench by the lake, the place where she went to cry after my father left, rendered in woodblock, went to a cousin; waters and skies to another cousin, to aunts and stepsiblings and in-laws and friends. I took home the roses she painted when she was young, and the sculpted likeness of the woman who was me, and the heads of women darkened with patina, the red clay torsos, the Renoir copy that had hung over the sofa, that my children wanted. I took the bronze dancer, a copy of a Degas we had seen the last time my mother had led my children and me through the museum, four months before she died.

Then I dispersed the glass paperweights my mother had collected, abstract worlds caught in globes, molten bubbles, veins of dye, nothing so overt as a scene. I gave away the tables and the chairs, their cushions stained; the beds, the lamps, the art supplies, some still untouched: brushes and gessoes and paints and craypas—most to my sister, some to my younger son who went to art school—

papers and rags; four closets full of clothing, plus still more: old crinolines and plaids and silks and tablecloths folded over rusting metal hangers in the basement. I took the shoes nested in tissue in their cardboard boxes; they fit me exactly, vintage, scarcely worn. My mother and I had the same feet. Our faces were similar enough to startle her friends, though hers held a different expression—a kind of openness that drew the attention of strangers. Our bodies were different—hers voluptuous, mine diminutive. I took the smaller jewels, necklaces in boxes, in plastic bags, strewn; and earrings, pins, and loose beads.

With my tiny aunt, I threw out drawers and shelves' worth of medicines—six or seven bottles of Tylenol, each with only a few pills gone, three or four bottles of Pepto Bismol, years-old prescriptions and current prescriptions—for high cholesterol, migraines, high blood pressure, thyroid, Leiden 5 clotting factor, pain, the inability to sleep. Those were just my mother's. My stepfather had pills too, and he had morphine; wrappers from something lay on the floor. My aunt held a black Hefty trash bag while I threw in medicinal casings, rubber gloves, ruined towels. Lotion. Mints. Toothpaste. Desiccated tissue. Lists, receipts. Pencil stubs, hair. In the drawers: bras, panties, hosiery, socks and peds, some never worn. (My stepfather's clothes we left for his kids.)

By the time we entered the kitchen with its food that was old now, its condiments and spices, its plastic ware and Tupperware and pots and pans and plastic bags and tin foil and napkins, I wanted the haulers to haul it away, as they would, in its entirety, the metal shelving unit in the garage with its used tools, turpentine, half-cans of paint, stained spades, nails, screws, the broken parts of things.

Instead, my aunt and I stood in front of the oven. We filled another Hefty bag, three. Then she retrieved the blue mug from a high shelf.

"Take it," she said.

"I don't need it," I said.

"Take it," she said.

"You'll enjoy it," she said. "You will."

I should mention that my aunt is not someone with whom one argues. Technically an ex-sister-in-law, she was one of my mother's closest friends. She had raised five kids, taught reading to children with learning disabilities, presided over the Milwaukee figure skating club. She sewed her own curtains. After my parents divorced, she had made it clear that my mother was to remain in my father's family's inner circle. What she said went.

I stuffed the mug in my carry-on, wrapped in some fabric I cannot recall. I went to UPS and sent myself boxes of things from that house, trucked cross-country in packing noodles and bubble wrap and shredded news and tape. I have a suitcase full of photographs and documents that I still have not opened, three years later.

The lines around my mother's lips have formed around my own. The blue mug—I use that every morning, drink my coffee before I wake my children up and set about to work.

My mother was visual; I am not. It took me years to notice that next to that triumphant, fractured blue bird, Picasso had painted a smaller bird, close enough to feel the larger's heat.

18   Dawn Raffel

The Moonstone Ring

My future husband bought the ring in India in 1981 with the idea that he would give it to the woman he married. Besides, he said, when he presented me with the ring in 1984, it was only $15. The ring is silver with a large moonstone flanked by blue. It was not my engagement ring—that was a quarter-carat perfect diamond. Anyway, the moonstone was too large. My fingers at the time were a child-sized four.

I took the moonstone ring to be sized. During the three days it was at the jeweler's, the 400-square foot apartment my future husband and I had just bought together in Chelsea was burglarized, and my jewelry, including the few pieces I owned that had belonged to my grandmother, was stolen. All I had left was my engagement ring, which was on my hand, and the moonstone ring in the shop.

In a few months, I also had a wedding band, and over the years my husband bought me jewelry, in part to make up for what I had lost. I rarely wore the moonstone—even properly sized, it seemed too big, too serious. Years went by; we moved from one apartment to another and out of Manhattan and had children. The diamond fell out of my engagement ring, never to be found, though the kids had a field day looking for it, pulling the cushions off furniture, sorting through the vacuum cleaner bag. I took off that ring with its empty prongs and thought about wearing the moonstone ring in its stead, but by now my knuckles had thickened and the ring was too small. So I returned it to the jeweler to be made bigger, only to be told it could not be sized again without destroying it.

The ring sat in my top drawer for more than a decade. During this time, a man in our small town opened a jewelry booth inside the liquor and soda store across from the takeout pizza joint, and I would occasionally browse while I waited for the kids' slices to heat. One day I was looking at a pair of earrings for my cousin when someone dropped off a ring to be sized. "Do you do that?" I said. "Sometimes," he said. I brought in the moonstone-and-blue-gem ring and he looked at it and said he thought he could enlarge it, despite what the more established jeweler had told me. Sure enough, he did.

So now, 29 years after my husband brought the ring from India, I wear it next to my wedding band. Those sapphires, the jeweler says, with some surprise, are real. The band slides over my knuckle, and the ring fits fine.

The Watch

The watch is a Bulova owned by my maternal grandfather, Bert Bern, né Bernat Beinenstok, a Hungarian immigrant who made his living selling Florsheim shoes and who, in his 92 years, had little taste for luxury. Frugal, he owned the same white car for all of my childhood, parked in the tiny lot behind the tiny Chicago apartment where he and my grandmother Elsie lived. I should be able to tell you the car's make but I can't, though I can tell you that before he quit smoking cigars and switched to endless packs of Wrigley's spearmint gum, you could suffocate in the back seat. And I can tell you that he loved little more than a heaving all-you-can-eat buffet because he'd gone hungry in childhood. (Go to a smorgasbord with him and he'd hector you relentlessly to have another dessert or three—"It's all the same price!") That he was sometimes mistaken for Mayor Richard Daley, Sr., to whom he bore a passing resemblance, pleased him.

When, after 49 years of marriage, my grand-mother Elsie died, he tracked down his childhood sweetheart, also named Elsie and by then widowed, and lived with her in California for the rest of his long life. It was as if his way of marking time was to rewind. He and Elsie #2—or #1, depending how you view it—bickered endlessly ("I'm not going to dial the phone for you when you go blind!" "Who's talking?!"), which was, I would like to think, a form of exercise. I watched him, at age 90, get into a screaming fight with his 92-year-old sister, who we were visiting in her assisted living facility, over who really brought their parents here from Kisvárda; they vowed never to speak again. ("Not another word to you!") After my grandfather marched us out, we stood on the curb in the 90-degree heat until our ride, Elsie's son, came to pick us up half an hour later. We had barely made it back to my grandfather and Elsie's tiny apartment before the phone rang; it was his sister. ("I watched you on the curb the whole time!") In the weeks before he died, my grandfather switched from heavily accented English ("Vot?") to his childhood Hungarian.

I couldn't tell you who gave him the Bulova watch but I will bet my own last hour that it was a gift. His heart failed finally—congestive disease. His only son had died two months before, and so the watch passed in pristine condition to his only grandson, Donald. Three years later, Donald went out for a run and died at 38.

The watch passed, via my mother, to my husband,

then ceased to tell time. Two repairs failed. For years my husband didn't wear any watch because, he said, he had one: It just didn't work. This year I bought him a Timex Expedition watch that tells not only the time and date but also the direction in which you are headed and when the local tides are coming in. For a few hundred dollars we could probably fix the Bulova watch for good. But I think my husband wants to outlive it.

The Lady on the Vase

One day when he was 101 years old, my Grandfather Raffel took the vase off the windowsill in his house and gave it to me. That vase had sat in the living room window for as long as I could remember. It is luminous blue, with an oval portrait of a lady painted on it.

He told me he'd bought the vase from the man moving out of the apartment into which my grandfather was moving his own young family. This was toward the end of the Depression. The man's wife had committed suicide. Desperate for cash, he was selling her things, including the vase, already antique, or at the least, old. My grandfather, who'd been poor himself, told me he bought it out of pity for that broken, broke man.

He handed it to me.

My grandfather died the following year at 102. ("It all went by so fast," he said, not long before he drew his final breath.)

The vase sits on the top shelf of my floor-to-ceiling bookcase—too high too reach, or break. Every day I see that face, surrounded by luminous blue. The woman is serene, young; her brown curls lustrous, falling as they may. Above a diaphanous gown, her bosom swells. She gives away nothing.

The Wedding Gift

The vase—blue, pottery—I guess blue is my color—was a gift from my college boyfriend. We'd drifted apart and become just friends for a few years and sometimes we wrote and sometimes we called and we invited each other to our weddings in cities four hours apart and neither of us went to the other's wedding and we sent each other presents. We mailed Christmas cards and then we didn't. When my husband and I were selling our last apartment in Manhattan, a woman who answered our ad turned out to be the roommate of the old boyfriend's sister, and I asked her to say hello and she said she would. The vase sat on the windowsill of my house for a long time, along with a whole collection of pottery and glass. When the kids were toddlers I put everything away, and now that they're older, I have other vases there.

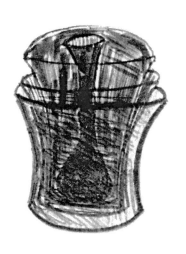

The Nesting Bowls

My mother bought the nesting bowls—four glass pieces that fit perfectly into each other's flared shape—shortly before her death. She called me from her cell phone to tell me that she had just placed them in blankets in the trunk of her car. She had bought them from the Hungarian woman who made them. ("She's 90 years old!" my mother said.) Even on her phone that was breaking up across the hundreds of miles between us, I could hear how happy my mother was about those bowls.

My mother kept the bowls—which aren't really bowls at all, and are not meant to contain anything save air, light and each other—on a mirror in the center of her dining room table. Their color is blue, close to cobalt. They are heavy.

I took the bowls when my mother died, shipped them wrapped in yards of protective material to my home, to my dining room table. The bowls could use a dusting. I have lost the pamphlet explaining the artist's work; in fact I don't remember the woman's name.

It's possible she's still alive.

The China Tree That Looks Like My Grandfather's China Tree

That we were Jewish didn't stop my family from pining after Christmas decorations. My parents would pile my sister and me into the car to drive around Milwaukee looking at displays of lights, Santas, reindeer, and angels. My Grandma Raffel hung stockings for us on her mantel. At Raffel's, the family furniture store, the Christmas tree was a business decision, my father said; customers expected it. The rule—unspoken but clearly conveyed—was, you didn't deny being Jewish but you didn't advertise it either. My sister and I would scheme, sometimes successfully, to be in the store on the day the tree was decorated, as a business decision.

My mother's family in Chicago was more overtly Jewish. While my Grandfather Raffel had been born into American poverty, Grandpa Bern had been raised a few hours from Budapest, one of seven children. His father had been a scholar, or, as my grandfather said bitterly, a man who never supported his family—although he did make and sell hand-turned wooden spice boxes and candlesticks, two of which I have. His mother was a milliner and grew the family's vegetables.

When I was 12, I made two attempts to get my grandfather to record his story, which my grandmother typed up on her manual typewriter (that later became my manual typewriter). The first version, beginning with "As per your request"— my grandmother's locution—had only to do with Jewish village life ("We had a parochial school where both Hebrew and Hungarian were taught... This was a fully accredited school, from which you could enter gymnasium after six years. This was compulsory, thanks to our King Franz Joseph..."). The second version told of leaving school at 13 to be apprenticed to a dry goods merchant. In 1913 he was to be drafted into the army in the service of Russia—"which resembles slavery," he wrote. It was illegal for him to leave, but he figured he'd choose capture over what he saw as certain death.

An old man who lived down the road from him, a cantor, bought a ticket and boarded a train to Germany, passed inspection, and in the last moment before the doors shut, jumped off the train, switching places with my grandfather, who was waiting on the platform. I do not know what befell that cantor. Most likely he survived the subterfuge—less likely the coming influenza epidemic and the war.

My grandfather, in an alternate route to the American immigrant dream, traveled by train across Europe, by ferry to Liverpool, by steamer to Canada, and by train to Chicago, where his older sister had already settled. (His American name— Bert Bern—was decided upon by his sister, her husband, and assorted cousins; he later said, with some bemusement, "I wasn't given a say.") In Chicago he worked a series of jobs, starting as floor sweeper, learned to write English mostly phonetically, and opened a Florsheim shoe store, if you will, on a shoestring. He told us years later that if he had not sold his entire inventory in his first week, he would not have been able to pay the rent, and would have been out of business.

My grandfather spent five days a week measuring men's feet with a metal slide and then going to the neat stacks of boxes in the back room to select the proper oxford or wingtip, pinching the toe box to check for optimal wiggle room. Any time he came to our house in Milwaukee, he would start his visit by examining our shoes, turning them over and over in his big red hands, grudgingly approving the saddle shoes, suspicious of the penny loafers, contemptuous of Keds ("Vot are these? You call these shoes?").

When it was our turn to visit Chicago, he would leave us with our grandmother on Saturday morning and walk alone to an old shul. Just as he refused ever to leave "The Blessed USA"—no visits to the old country for him, no sir, and you could keep Paris and London too—he refused to forget that he was a Hungarian Jew. His accent clung to him. (His favorite word was "alamash!"—I am not sure what this meant in his native tongue but over the years it became an all-purpose imperative for anything from "Let's go!" to "Change the subject!" to "Enough already!" and, on occasion, "Let's eat!") He believed in ritual. Visit at Passover and you were likely to pass out before the prayers ended and the food was served.

My grandfather's concession to American Christmas was to place in the store a small glazed porcelain tree that plugged into an outlet, kindling its colored lights. My mother loved that tree. She ferreted it home to Milwaukee when my grandfather closed the store for the last time—though it never left the basement. My sister has it now.

My husband met my grandfather just once, during what was both the summer before our wedding and the final summer of my grandfather's life. In L.A. on business, Mike took my grandfather and his wife, Elsie, out to dinner.

"What are you having, Bert?" Elsie said.

"You know I can't read the menu!" he said. "I'm waiting for you to tell me!"

If my 91-year-old grandfather was close to blind, Elsie's vision wasn't much better. And though her hearing was fine, she had developed the habit of shouting to penetrate my grandfather's near-deafness. Not far from their table, my husband said, was a woman in a low-cut dress. "Look, Bert," Elsie yelled as they were winding up their meal, "she's naked!" My grandfather let Elsie walk out of the restaurant ahead of him and took his Irish Catholic future son-in-law, whose wedding he would not live to see, by the arm. "Let's go back," he said to Mike, "and have another look."

We named our first child for him. (Given that my grandfather had changed his name from Bernard to Bert, I felt justified in changing it to Brendan.)

Every year at Christmas, my husband and our sons, Brendan and Sean, drive north to the woods to cut down a tree, which we decorate with boxes of ornaments and yards and yards of lights, including the bubbling 1950s kind from his parents' house. We have an angel in the window, stockings on the stairs, and three menorahs in the kitchen. We also have a china tree from CVS, one-foot high, with tiny bulbs, just like the one my grandfather had.

The Tea Set From Japan

My father was stationed on Guam during World War II. He'd been an engineering student at Marquette University at the time the war broke out. When he was drafted, the army sent him for advanced training at Harvard—the big band leader, Glenn Miller, who would die overseas, used to play for the troops during drills—and then, with the top two percent of his Harvard class, to the rad lab at MIT. He landed on Guam with the initial deployment from the Air Corps, and was part of the team who built the first radar.

Unknown to anyone, my father had a congenital, degenerative disease of the middle ear that caused his hearing to be destroyed by the noise on the air base where he serviced warplanes. By the time he visited Japan after the armistice, he was functionally deaf and would remain so for almost 20 years. He used a large hearing aid that whistled feedback until the early 1960s when the ruined bones of his middle ear were replaced with Teflon. Nevertheless, at the time he visited Japan, he perceived an unrestricted future; he was about to return home from war and begin a career in aeronautics, for which he'd developed a passion.

My father had some of the most advanced training in the world, but he had underestimated the degree of anti-Semitism in this country after the war, especially in the engineering field. He received one job offer, which was rescinded after he filled out a form in which he was asked to state his religion. (My father's uncle, faced with the same problem, changed his name, moved to another city, joined a church, became an engineer, and never told his new family he was Jewish. My sister remembers going to his daughter's wedding as a child and being sworn to secrecy on the topic of religion; years later, one of his granddaughters tracked me down online, trying to learn her family history.)

My father went to work, wearing his hearing aid, in his father's family furniture store; he spent his days selling LazyBoy recliners and Philco appliances and Lane end tables, and his spare time in the basement on his homemade ham radio, communicating, often in Morse Code, with people thousands of miles away (his call signal was W9QCJ and I can still recall him saying it—"Queen, Charlie, Japan") and reading up on physics and astronomy. All that remained of my father's war years were the rank-smelling uniforms hanging in the basement and the red tea set.

I don't think my father was especially unhappy;

he was someone who could coax an adventure from just about any set of circumstances. (Some of his escapades were less than practical. The $19 inflatable boat deflated in Lake Michigan; we swam back. Allowing me, at nine, to steer the Cessna he had rented in exchange for a loveseat nearly resulted in loop-de-loop; we never told my mother.) After his hearing was restored, he adored music and dance. But there was always, for the rest of his life, I thought, a shadow, or a hint of disturbance— something sensed in a stray aside or silence.

At some point he gave the tea set to me. Now it sits in my china cabinet. To the best of my knowledge, it has never been used.

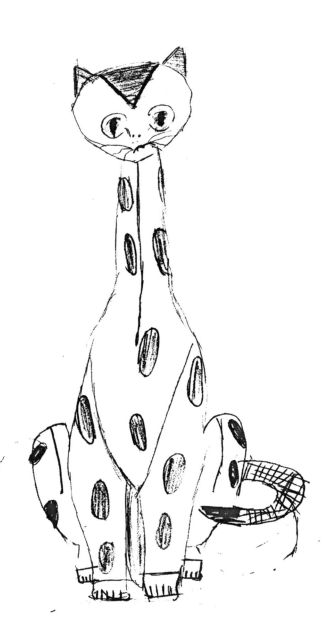

The Cat

The black and white china cat sat on my Grandmother Raffel's window ledge all the years she was an invalid. The cat seemed to watch the world through glass. When she was younger, my grandmother raised two boys, kept the books for the family furniture store, held office at half the clubs in town, melted her silver down for the war, survived the telegram telling her one of her sons was badly injured (it was my uncle, who'd broken his back parachuting out of a burning plane; his cousin would soon be dead), read the entire library of Reader's Digest condensed books, entertained her many friends often and enthusiastically despite being—forgive me—an inattentive cook (she burned frozen entrees by forgetting them in the oven; neglected to buy ingredients for baking and substituted anything at hand, such as Smucker's jelly for cake frosting; made Jell-O molds that failed to gel and wept in festive red and green and yellow pools on platters, forlorn chunks of fruit bobbing up...nobody came for the food). She thought nothing of taking three or four or five of her grandchildren to an amusement park for the day, or out for Chinese New Year, such as it was in Milwaukee in the 1960s, (neon drinks adorned with paper parasols; celery-heavy chop suey), or on a boat ride, or to the theater (she insisted on front row seats) or to hear music under the stars. I have two pictures of my grandmother. In one, she is striding purposefully down the street while snapped in a 1930s candid, her gaze intent and confident; in another, she is in a rowboat with my grandfather and she is the one rowing. She wielded fierce opinions on everything from politics (she cast an absentee ballot for Richard Nixon, then died of a heart attack the week before the election) to hot pants on girls (she was in favor and wanted to know why I wasn't wearing them).

By her late sixties, she was largely confined by heart disease to her house. On Sunday nights, she marked up the *TV Guide* for the week—talk shows, news, no soaps. My grandfather continued to work, long past retirement age, in the furniture store, and to sneak out on occasion in the evenings to the Big Boy for strawberry pie. The phone rarely rang.

My grandmother's last few years went in a circuit from the bed to the TV chair to the kitchen and back to the bed. "They shoot horses, don't they," she said.

I had the cat on top of my china cabinet when my older son, born 30 years after her death, asked me about it. Then he reached up for the cat and put it in the window, facing out.

The Jewelry Box

The children's nanny was the other woman in my house. D came from Trinidad, one of nine children; her own mother, she told me, had married at 14. (I interviewed many nannies and will confess now that what clinched the deal was not only D's abundant warmth and her enthusiastic references but also her answer when I asked: What do babies dream about? Several nanny candidates were flummoxed by that. D's answer, without missing a beat, was that her mother told her babies dream of angels— which told me that D didn't find unanswerable questions irksome or absurd.) Although she was not much older than I, her daughter was in college (and would become a lawyer); her son was 10 and in school.

Because D knew my children in the most intimate way, knew the way they smelled as babies, the feel of their skin, the heft of their bodies— asleep, awake, jumping—she seemed to know my heart. And she certainly knew my house, its needs and its wants and its lapses. She knew I kept my jewelry in a battered old box that I didn't bother to replace, the way I didn't bother to replace so many old and broken things when there was so much to be bought and done for and taught to the children. In nine years she missed maybe four days of work—unless it was Divali, when she would bring over fragrant Indian food, roti and samosas and fish wrapped in foil. She spoiled my children and loved them too, and her husband ruined their appetites by bringing them candy and chips before dinner. She was surely more patient than I, and quicker to laugh, and better at artful arrangements of just about anything. I never wanted our arrangement—this feminine partnership in my home—to end, but of course it had to; the children were in school all day. She left the month after my mother died.

Now she calls and I call and we visit and she remembers the day my father died and the way the kids both daydream (one on his feet, the other with his pencil) but it's not the same. The chair she liked to sit in most is broken. She was better than I am, my children remind me, at making Cream of Wheat and also singing. I miss her easy laughter and her lilting Island voice. I keep my finest jewels in the box she bought for me.

The Rug

While my Grandfather Bern's tastes were simple, my Grandmother Bern liked elegant old things and she would go to auctions to find them—end tables and porcelain urns and pretty rugs and lamps. By the time my grandparents were moving from the apartment where they'd raised my mother and uncle to a one-bedroom, my grandmother had amassed a collection of real Oriental rugs that she couldn't take with her.

My mother didn't want them. She liked everything modern: white leather, white carpet, chrome and glass. And so the only rug that stayed in the family was a tiny Oriental rectangle that sat under my grandmother's tea cart at the mouth of her galley kitchen. The cart was used to hold dishes to be brought to the little eating nook or to wheel demi-glasses of tomato juice with lemon out to the metal folding table set up in the living room for Thanksgiving dinner.

My grandmother loved to cook and bake—from that cramped kitchen emerged paprika chicken with mushrooms and rice, lamb chops with jelly, key lime pie, lemon meringue, pineapple

strudel, sponge cake and chocolate cake, layered
and frosted and studded with walnuts. She would
feed us and fuss, and each time we said goodbye,
tears welled in her eyes. Sometimes she would
mail us food she'd made.

My mother put cooking in the same box as
old furniture and religious ritual—something
oppressive, from a generation where women were
subservient. She liked to remind me that her own
grandmother had died of a heart attack while
standing in a hot kitchen making Rosh Hashanah
dinner. She would point out her mother's ankles
swelling over the tops of her shoes as she stood
at the counter chopping nuts or over the burner
boiling dumplings. My mother wanted out
with the old—the old country ways, old habits,
obligations, dark and heavy furnishings, things
that looked traditional or, worse, antique. Still,
after my grandmother died and my grandfather
moved out to California, my mother brought home
that tiny rug, and she often lamented that she'd
let the others go. She brought home her mother's
monogrammed purses (her own initials, always,
not those of some designer), her gloves, her pinned
hats. Her glassware and dishes, although they were
heavily chipped. Her ornate gold watch, which my
mother never wore ("After I die," my mother said,
"take it to New York and sell it." But my sister

wanted it, although she never wears it either.) I believe those rugs were the only things she had given away and wished she'd had back. The sole remaining one went in my mother's downstairs bathroom—there really wasn't any other place for it in her white/glass/chrome suburban townhouse. It got threadbare.

Emptying my mother's desk and dresser drawers after her death, I found notes everywhere, addressed to me and to my sister, having to do with what she wanted done with her possessions. Some of these notes must have been 20 years old, judging by the faded ink and by the fact that they referred to people long deceased as if they were alive. Some were more recent. All where handwritten. One of them instructed me to take the Oriental rug.

I had given that rug no thought at all and had no idea what to do with it. But here was my mother, dead, and still talking to me. I didn't dare leave it, didn't dare give it away. Right now the rug is under the desk in the office where I write.

The Mexican Fisherman

When my father left my mother, he started to travel. The metal sculpture of the fisherman from Mexico was a divorce appeasement gift to me. I was 15 and angry—with pretty much everyone. And yet, that sculpture followed me to umpteen dormitory rooms and apartments, walk-ups, sublets, roach motels.

Now they are both dead, my father and my mother. And I still love that fisherman, waiting for the catch.

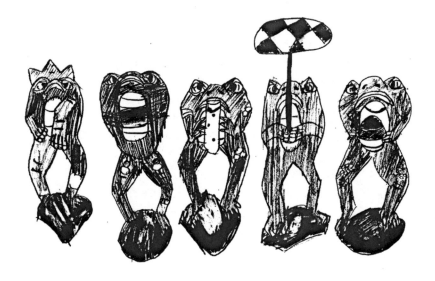

The Frogs

My husband saw me looking in the window of a store at five wooden Balinese frogs, each playing a musical instrument. A week later, on our anniversary, those frogs were on our bed. This is why we're married.

French Bowls

My first job in New York was at a magazine where a frail, elderly man delivered the interoffice mail. Over time it emerged that he was an artist and had in fact made the spare, expressive paintings that were hanging in the magazine's corridors. He spoke very little but I often noticed him looking intently at me. Once I heard him say, "Very French."

One day he dropped off a drawing at my desk, told me that he had made it for me and walked away, embarrassed. The drawing, rendered in just a few dark strokes, was of a woman's face, and though it was not particularly representational, there was something unnervingly familiar in the cast of her eyes and the set of her mouth.

I left the magazine soon afterward and never saw that man again. A few years later, my future husband took one look at the drawing, which I'd had framed, and said, "That is definitely you."

We went to Paris for our honeymoon and again for our twentieth anniversary. Leaving our hotel in the Place St. Germain every morning, we passed a pottery shop. In the window was a set of bowls; painted inside each was a woman's face that looked to me strikingly like the face in the drawing hanging over the fuse box at home. I said nothing about it. After we'd walked past a few more times, my husband said, "It's odd, isn't it, seeing your young face in that window."

We went in and bought the bowls.

The Prayer Book

I have very little belonging to my father, who died of a heart attack in the middle of a ballroom dance class. (After his quadruple bypass, he liked to dance to "Stayin' Alive," although he also favored Latin rhythm. At the funeral, the old folks were jealous.) My stepmother dispensed with the bulk of his belongings—the effects, as they say. I don't know where they went. But not long after his death, she led me to a small drawer in their house by the lake, explaining that he had told her it was his private stuff, and he didn't want her looking there. She asked me to empty it out.

I opened the drawer wondering what could be so secret. Inside I found things like batteries and the directions for the Code-a-Phone answering machine. A lanyard and a wallet I had made for him at camp, with his initials burnt awkwardly into the leather. A keychain my mother had given him on the occasion of my sister's wedding as a sort of token. An autobiography, typed, stapled—school assignment—written when he was 16 years old. And the thing that shocked me—a prayer book, inscribed to him on his Bar Mitzvah by his paternal grandparents. I'd had no idea that father had even had a Bar Mitzvah. No one in the family had ever mentioned it, and my grandparents did not belong to a synagogue. My father would cheerfully describe himself as a born-again atheist; if you happened to be sitting next to him during a service to which my mother had dragged him, you could hear him muttering "baloney" under his breath.

Yet I don't think he kept the prayer book solely out of attachment to his grandparents. True, I did wonder whether he was laughing from the beyond when I went to a synagogue each week to recite the mourner's Kaddish, the prayer of the bereaved. He believed deeply in science. He talked, despite his professed atheism, about the divinity of subatomic connection, and he told me once that he believed the infinite resided in the infinitesimal. He approached nature with awe. On a postcard sent to me from South America, he wrote only, "I've learned that A SPIDER IS NOT AN INSECT!!! Love, Dad."

Spiders, he respected—ritual, not much. Several times he told me the story of the lost cousin— the child who died because my father's uncle had insisted on going through with a bris in a room full of coughing people, even though the baby was sickly and frail. "What a waste," my father said again and again. And yet, for all his distaste for organized religion, I don't think he could ever be shut of his blood, of his bones, his genes.

The prayer book is old-school, insistent on the literal resurrection of the dead, where more reform prayer books lean toward the idea that the dead live on in the living. For a year or so after my father died, I couldn't stop reading books about death, by medieval mystics and postmodern intellectuals, by those who believe in reincarnation and those convinced that what comes next is nothing at all. A smidgen of carbon. Maybe, I thought, my father would have liked the death of death theory, which rejects the whole paradigm. At one point, he'd toyed with having his head frozen, freaking out my stepmother. Instead, he'd been cremated. The ashes were buried under a tree, in a cardboard box, in a nature preserve, whether legally or not I do not know.

The prayer book is in my dresser drawer.

The Bride's Bible

My mother received the bible the day she married
my father. It is small, white, leather-bound, gilded
at the edges. She never left home overnight without
it. That bible was tucked into her suitcase, even if
she was going for just a night. It traveled with her to
her parents' apartment in Chicago and on the sales
incentive trips to Bermuda and the Bahamas and
Hawaii and Puerto Rico that my father received for
selling sufficient quantities of Philco appliances at
Raffel's Furniture Store. It went up the Wisconsin
peninsula for our three-day, retail-family vacations
(my father was always on call) and down to the
southern end of Indiana where her brother lived,
and out to California when her father moved
there with Elsie #2. The bible moved out of one
marriage and into another. It went to hotel rooms
in New York, in Dallas, in London, in Paris, and
in sleepy towns in Michigan, Wisconsin, Illinois….
It went in cars and vans and planes and buses and
ferries and shuttles and trains and sedans. It got
fat, with handwritten prayers and sayings stuck
under its covers on paper scraps. It went on cruises
for retirees and also to hospital rooms.

I wanted the bible to go in the coffin with my mother, but my stepfather and sister thought it belonged to the living world. I've slipped it next to my father's prayer book.

The Lock

In my nightstand there is a small white envelope holding a single golden ringlet. It came from Brendan's first haircut. Now his hair is thick and dark and coarse like mine. He is tall and deep-voiced. When he was smaller, he kept a little box, like a treasure, of his jewel-like baby teeth. Whether he keeps it still, I do not know. I held onto my own yanked teeth for years and years. Some people cherish relics, finding divinity in a fleshless finger bone. Why do we cling to the body's pieces, as if they can tell us who we are, and what was lost, and how time passed?

The Rocking Chair

It was my sister's first and then mine—the wooden chair that played a lullaby, the work of a pin that triggered the components in a metal box when it rocked. This chair was the seat of our dreams. Hours, I sat lost in thought before the age of video, computer, enrichment. The chair became Brendan's and then Sean's. Slowly it broke, the music box first (repaired, re-broken), and then— the work of boys in the house, of time on wood— the arms, the rocking pieces. I couldn't bear to look. It's safe to say my husband took the chair away, but I never did ask. Once when I was cleaning out the toy bin I found a broken piece of it and held it in my hand, as if it could rock me back into my past as I imagine it.

The Sewing Box

I keep my needles and threads in a small round cardboard box that was originally home to a jigsaw puzzle given to me by my Grandmother Bern. The box showed how the 36-piece puzzle would look when assembled, with two teary pink heart-faces floating in red and pink paisley. The pieces have vanished and the box is mostly broken, disconnecting at its seams.

My mother stored her needles and threads, and buttons and snaps, hooks, eyes, her cloth tomato full of pushpins, and her measuring tape in a Barton's bonbonnier tin ("Continental Chocolates") from the 1950s, with stylized icons of the world's great places—the Kremlin, Big Ben. The lid barely shut. She had decades-old darning needles packaged by Singer, 30 cents for six. Her threads told the story of the colors she favored—reds and blues, black, plums, pinks, flower colors, summer shades, but no green, for which she expressed an inexplicable dislike.

When the time came to bury my mother, my stepfather asked me to pick a dress. He seemed to think I could complete this task in under ten minutes—he was one of the most practical, decisive men I've ever met, even—or especially—during the months when he was dying. It was hard for him, I think, to understand second-guessing. My mother, however, had four closets full of clothes for me to chose from, plus more in the basement. She never left the house without the right shoes, the right bag, the perfect accessories; if I screwed this up, I thought, she'd come back to haunt me.

I wanted my mother in death to look beautiful and elegant and like the artist that she was, but not as if she were going off to a cocktail party in the hereafter. I wasn't entirely sure which garments fit; she kept three sizes. Standing in front of cashmeres and silks and brushed cottons, I was paralyzed. One jacket that she hadn't, I was sure, worn in years reduced me to tears. I can't even say what it made me remember.

Then I saw a simple cotton-blend sheath with cutouts at the neckline and delicate beading in blue and pink and lavender. I'd never seen it on her. I looked at the label, which said FAITH. I added taupe heels, a glass heart necklace from her beloved art museum. She didn't need a bag but in the eleventh hour my stepfather and I tucked a packet of her ubiquitous Kleenex tissue into the coffin.

I found the Barton's candy box the next year, after my stepfather died. Amid the orphaned threads, the threaded needles, pins, I saw the extra buttons to the dress, attached to the cardboard price tag that said FAITH.

And so I have two sewing boxes, though I rarely use them. The long-lost puzzle that my grandmother gave me had dialogue under those campy, weepy hearts: "I don't miss you. I have something in my eye."

The Dress

The sleeveless jersey dress is far beyond repair. It's stained. It doesn't fit. The fabric has faded. Goodwill would not want it. I keep it in my closet because it holds in its weave the summer of 1984: the heat, my young body, the necklace—all hearts—that I wore with it that broke, our rooftop in twilight, the city below us, the promise of the life I planned to live. That dress was so green.

Mr. and Mrs. Buttercream

The couple from the top of the wedding cake is sitting, or rather standing, on top of the dresser, next to the coins and the answering machine, which is blinking again, the jewelry box, the blue glass lamp. They're poised for rice, or birdseed. The dress is discolored. That dress was so white.

The Teacup

At 20, I went to visit my closest friend from college during her junior year in London. We had been roommates in the Midwest, but she'd gone overseas and I had transferred to an East Coast college where I realized that, yes, there is a class system in America and, yes, I was outclassed. I sensed unspoken rules that I didn't understand. I had spent my summers waitressing and hostessing at places with names like Mr. Steak and—for one especially demeaning week before I was fired for a lethal combination of incompetence and a reprehensible attitude—serving overpriced chops while wearing a uniform that involved a plastic miniskirt and a holster. My classmates, meanwhile, had apparently spent their summers interning in Senator Kennedy's office. Imagine my surprise when I discovered that I had an accent. I was eager to escape for Christmas break and equally eager not to go back to Wisconsin where, during those pre-climate change years, the temperature often dipped below minus-20, and where my parents' post-divorce relations remained somewhat chilly.

Freddy Laker's airline, with service from New

York to London, was as cheap as it got. They didn't sell tickets in advance (you had to show up and wait), or serve food on board (not even micro-pretzels), and the original seats had been removed so that smaller, cheaper ones could be wedged in. (I weighed 90 pounds dripping wet; I can't imagine how someone larger must have felt). Everyone smoked. It was like crossing the Atlantic in an ashtray—in my case, next to a woman who wanted to describe to me all the way over the ocean how plants talked to her. I can't remember what they said.

C met me at Heathrow. She had gone punk. She had also discovered that if you told Londoners that you were an American journalist and, I suppose, at least as importantly, if you were an attractive young woman, you could get backstage at any concert. ("We're going to hear the Boomtown Rats and after that there's an all-night party," she announced at the airport, but an hour later when I fell down half a flight of stairs due to jetlag, I decided I'd better sit that one out). To earn money, C worked at a pub where her fellow beer puller, Mrs. Lydon, was Johnny Rotten's mother.

The reality, though, is that we were Midwestern girls gorging on our temporary freedom, much the way my grandfather indulged at a buffet. While punk and rage called us, so did high tea and crumpets, clotted cream and white gloves. Conventional wisdom has it that at 20 you don't know who you are, but I think I understood, at the very least, who I wasn't, and that I had better visit while I could the worlds—punk, high tea—to which I would never belong. I understood, as well, the world I didn't want to live in: my mother's. For all that I didn't fit in at an East Coast school, I didn't fit either in the Wisconsin of the 1960s and 1970s —too bookish, too dark-haired, too oddly dressed, too slow to smile. It wasn't until I first laid eyes on Greenwich Village, six months after London, that I recognized, for the first time, a place where I belonged. In a neighborhood where everyone appeared to be a misfit, I could fit right in.

The teacup was a gift from C to me. She bought it at Harrod's: a single, expensive, floral china cup with a saucer to match. That I have never drunk from it, and that I still have it, and that C is my closest friend 31 years later, says something, I think, about a woman's education, or maybe only us.

Rose-Colored Glasses

I met L in London when I went to visit C. She was a theater major who ended up dropping out of school to go to New York and act. Right after graduation, C and I moved to New York too, with the idea that we would both get glamorous jobs as assistants at magazines. That this plan worked (although the glamour part amounted to accepting invitations, palmed off on us by our bosses, to luncheons at Tavern on the Green and 21, where in return for a chicken cutlet we were required to sit through mind-blowingly boring pitches for products the magazine was never going to feature; we also occasionally rubbed elbows with well-known authors who were slumming by writing for "the glossies"—one sent C, in the envelope with his typewritten manuscript, an invoice for the stamp)—that we quickly found jobs as well as an apartment was a tribute both to the times and to the dumb luck of the naïve. We lived in the heart of the Village, and everyone we knew was a writer or an actor or an artist with a day job. We saw L all the time.

In 1979, New York was dirty and dangerous. (I

used to contend that my mother believed the Certain Death Zone was anything beyond the nine-block stretch between the Plaza Hotel and Saks, although she loved the Village Halloween parade—"Wait! Is that a man or a woman?" I couldn't get her to leave, despite the freezing weather; the only ones wearing dresses that day were men.) You could live in the Village on next to nothing (which was what C and I earned) as long as you didn't mind walking up seven flights, or having your bathtub in the kitchen, or hearing your upstairs neighbors play their Hammond organ at three in the morning, or your downstairs neighbors party and brawl, or someone dropping weights on the floor next door, or, for that matter, sneezing, and as long as you weren't overly perturbed by roaches and mice in the kitchen, and junkies, trannies, and hookers in the street. (An actor friend of my future husband lived on Avenue D; one night we went back to his place to find a dead mouse splayed out on the floor next to a scrap of paper. We speculated that the neighborhood was so bad that even the mice were committing suicide.) You could nurse one cheap cup of coffee at the Figaro all night (we used to have contests to see who could sit in the café longest without ordering anything—the winning time was 42 minutes—or fill up on kasha varnishkas at the Veselka, or the dense vegetable soup and challah at the Kiev where the elderly Ukrainians coexisted nonchalantly with kids with green hair and safety pins through their noses, or go dancing at the Ritz, where you might get in free wearing a miniskirt and, if not, there was always some Wall Street guy happy to pick up the tab for you and six of your closest friends, or listen to music at Max's Kansas City, where there was always the possibility that someone might vomit on you, or catch a revival movie at the Bleecker Street Theater, where the projector broke at least once during every showing and the floor stuck to your feet, or take in an off-off-off Broadway show or showcase—L acted in a lot of those. We heard Spalding Gray perform in The Garage in Soho (L said, "You've got to hear this guy") and a teenage Whitney Houston sing with her mother at the Bottom Line. Often we'd end up eating pneumatic muffins at four or five in the morning at the Triumph on Bleecker—we were young enough to do that and still get up a few hours later, and go to work.

When Mike and I got married, C and L gave us six blushing pink-stemmed wine glasses because, they said, they wanted us always to see through rose colored glasses. (C and L held the bachelorette party in L's East Village walkup; her roommate, an aspiring comedian, was one of the funniest people we'd ever heard—until she got onstage in front of strangers, and then she froze.)

Over the years Mike and I have had some serious attrition of wine and water glasses, champagne flutes and snifters, steins and liqueur glasses, and carafes and pitchers, as well as plates large and small, cups and saucers, platters, most of the soup bowls, the butter dish in shards. But those six glasses have survived intact.

C is still my closest friend. L stopped acting, went back to school and moved to Brooklyn—not so far away at all—but once there was a half-hour train ride, I saw her less and less. The last time I was with L was New Year's Day at the end of the 1980s; we talked and laughed and ate and couldn't have known that we wouldn't see each other again.

If you think this is a story with a climactic or heartrending ending, it isn't. We just never got around to making plans. We spoke a few times on the phone. Years later I ran into a mutual acquaintance and asked after L, and we said we should all get together, and we didn't. We had young kids then and full-time jobs, households, commutes. After awhile, so much time had passed that it would have felt strange to call. Where to begin? Before we knew it, 20 years went by.

I wonder sometimes what we'd have said to each other if we'd understood that it was the last time, just as I wonder how it would have been if

I had known that rushed phone call while I was trying to put dinner on the table on a Monday night would be the final time I spoke to my father, or if I had recognized the night—I can't even remember it—that was the last time I would pick up one of my sleeping sons and carry him to bed.

Sometimes things shatter. More often they just fade.

Soap

I met A at a colloquium in Paris in 2007. She stood out among the French academics and their American guests both because of her flamboyant manner of dress—many colors, none muted—and her boundless exuberance. Over dinner I learned that while I had been sitting in cafes in Greenwich Village in the 1980s, A was escaping Romania, saying a covert goodbye to her parents. ("Don't be worried," she told me she'd said, "if you don't hear from me again.") She'd wanted to live in America but had gone first to France, not realizing that you can seek asylum only once. She'd had trouble getting her writing published in part, she said, because she wrote and thought in three languages: Romanian, French, and English. Her English was flawless.

One day we snuck out of the colloquium into the gray relentless rain of Paris in March to go to a designer sample sale, trying on clothes and buying nothing, and again to escape the university lunch of water crackers with microscopic bits of meats and cheeses, and off to a café where we ordered giant salads drowning in crème fraiche. For three days we were best friends. She vowed she was coming to visit New York in the fall, though I knew, and suspect she did too, that she wouldn't. Sometimes we email. Before I left Paris, she handed me a cellophane-wrapped soap with an exuberant daisy in the middle. I keep it on my dresser; it's too good to wash with.

Seconds

When the children were small, almost every night when the weather was good, or simply good enough, I used to meet three other women in the park. We met around seven, after work. Our husbands were working later than we were—two were chefs in restaurant kitchens half the night. Exhausted from babies and toddlers and jobs and laundry and dishes that did not end, we'd heave our kids into the baby swings and push them and push them and pull them out—Brendan's toddler cowboy boots would catch in the swing's leg holes—and help them up ladders and into and out of wide plastic tunnels and chase them as they chased after fireflies across the open lawn. These weren't the alpha moms who would soon appear in town, angling their $800 strollers into the new Starbucks. We dressed in sweats and leggings and oversized Ts. No one worked in publishing, as I did, or trafficked in words. These were women who, had my children been born in an ever so slightly different time or place, I would never have met: a chef, a chef, a caterer/potter. I think they saved my life.

We'd stay until well after darkness fell in the park or else leave to get what might have been the world's worst pizza (fake cheese, tasteless—but the owner tolerated, with minimal dirty looks, our noise and detritus). One Christmas eve, two of the women, with their husbands who were, for once, not working in restaurants, converged at our house. (Imagine the pressure of cooking for that many professional chefs—in an act of cowardice, I let my husband do it.) The five kids under six didn't last long at the table, seized as they were by the kind of anticipatory frenzy that is usually only possible in the very young. I'm sure there was a great mess and that we were dead tired, but what I remember are the children shrieking in delight. I also remember the other two women, trained in restaurant kitchens, converging on mine like a SWAT team; I have never seen anyone deep-clean anything so fast.

What happened in the following year was school. Boys played with boys, and girls with girls. We had homework now, and sensible bedtimes. C, the potter, moved farther than walking distance, to a house where she had her own kiln. Little by little, the park nights stopped.

The other three women are now divorced. K left town. T, I see rarely—we wave when we pass. Every so often, though, I hang out with C, the potter whose skinny boy is now a well-built, tall young man. We lost a mutual friend last year, at 50, to cancer, a woman whose son is the same age as ours. C still throws in her kiln-equipped basement—bowls, vases, and dishes that she sells in Manhattan. I've bought several of her graceful blue and green serving pieces. But C knows the ones I like best are the $5 seconds—the ones she can't sell in stores: The glaze has dripped and bubbled, the clay shows in patches, the color, when baked, turned wonderfully strange. Perfection is sometimes the enemy of good. Besides, I like a lucky accident.

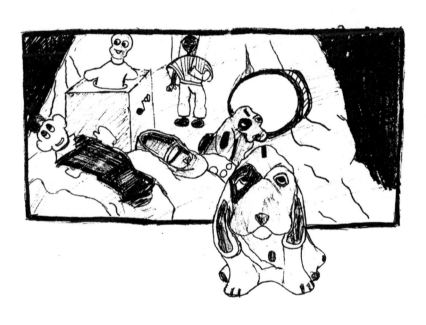

The Florsheim Dog

My mother painted a still life in acrylic of my toys when I was four: a marionette, a red-and-white striped tin drum, a jack-in-the-box from which the clown had sprung, a pink ballet slipper—though I have no recollection of taking ballet at that age—and the Florsheim dog, all set against the backdrop of my blue baby blanket. The dog, a gray, long-eared, adorably dolorous hound, was the logo for the Florsheim shoes that my grandfather sold; this particular Florsheim dog was not a toy but a piggy—or doggie—bank. It was plastic, covered in some indeterminate fuzzy material. I kept my pennies there. A few stray pennies are spread on the blanket in the painting.

My mother's composition went into storage from the time I was around nine until Brendan was born. Until recently it hung in the room he shared with Sean. Occasionally, I'd ask whether they were ready for me to take it down; they weren't. We put it away only when we were starting renovation of that room.

About a year before she died, my mother called to say that she had found the Florsheim dog, only a little broken, in her basement, and that she was mailing it to me. She seemed to feel that I would be delighted by this news. Of the physical dog, which was cracked, and which my mother had stuffed with plastic bags to prevent it from caving in while in transit, I had no first-hand memory— my only memory was of an image fixed in time, a portion of my mother's rendition of my childhood. The painting expressed not so much who I was by way of my possessions as who I was in the eyes of my mother, suffused, I can assume, with who she wished I was: the work not only of her genes and tutelage but also of her desire. The whole of the composition was more than the sum of the toys; it was a portrait of a child who had, for a moment, stepped away.

Eventually, in cleaning out the boxes in the basement of my mother's house, I found the toy drum too. I was not surprised that Sean, who was past the age of playing with such things, wanted it. The drum belongs to his childhood as much as to mine, proof of the truth of the image, a residue of who his mother was, by way of his grandmother's eyes.

The painting is stored in my basement now, covered by sheets, as if shrouded, until, perhaps, I have a grandchild who might like it.

As for the Florsheim dog, it's sitting on my

nightstand, a loyal, broken guardian—not of my dreams but of my mother's vision of what they might have been.

94   Dawn Raffel

Rascal

My mother and sister were having a mother-daughter art show in Milwaukee. My sister, who was living outside of Dallas, had dozens of her watercolors shipped north and framed. My mother went through her studio and attic, making choices from a lifetime's work of oil, acrylic, watercolor, and sculpture. I flew in for the opening with my sons, who were then two and five. (Of greatest interest to the children were the platters of dainty cookies—my mother felt no event was complete without them, including any reading I ever gave in Milwaukee. These sugary confections with their tough red cherry centers took me back to the stale consolations of my childhood, waiting for my mother to finish—finally, finally—at whatever gallery over which she was presiding).

The mother-daughter show was attended mostly by our Raffel cousins, my aunt and my uncle, and by my mother's enormous network of friends. My mother had "best girlfriends" dating back to grammar school in Chicago, through every stage of her childhood and adulthood and, as people retired, in all the warmer parts of the country: Florida, the geriatric towns in California, New Mexico, Arizona.

My sister's evocative watercolors—some of nature, others more abstract, even quilt-like—were familiar to me. I had seen the bulk of them before, and those that I hadn't seen correlated so directly to my own interiority that I felt I already knew them. Many of her paintings sold that day.

My mother's work was also mostly known to me, save for a dark, moody landscape that looked like a place one might remember only briefly after waking. It was nothing like the paintings—brighter, more primary, more insistent on good cheer—that I had seen throughout all of my childhood, and it turned out to have been a survivor of her high school studies at the Art Institute in Chicago. It seemed to represent some animate part of my mother that I had always sensed and that, I felt, she had tried to suppress. It refused to be nice. Even a charcoal drawing of her own mother, my Grandmother Bern, lying in her coffin (believe me, this was not on display, and she had been reprimanded for it by some of her fellow art students in Milwaukee, who found it unnecessarily morbid), held, to my eyes, a certain degree of politeness.

My father had once incensed my mother by commenting that she'd been a better artist before she earned an art degree, at the University of

Milwaukee, while I was in grade school. But here was evidence that his assessment, if not kind, was not entirely untrue.

Only one of my mother's paintings sold that day, and I am heartbroken to report that it was that impassioned landscape, for hundreds of dollars. An acquaintance of hers, someone I didn't know, bought it. I lacked the courage to say that I wanted that image, that view of my mother's psyche, for myself.

After the show, the family went out to a restaurant that had a game arcade where the kids could play while we ate bargain Continental cuisine. I went to check on Sean and found him mesmerized in front of a man playing a game in which you insert a dollar and have 30 seconds or so to capture a stuffed dog with a metal crane. Into the crane and down the chute came a big brown canine prize of indeterminate breed while my son watched with unadulterated longing. I watched as the man turned and saw Sean and, without a word, handed him the dog. And I watched Sean's expression change from longing to the look of someone who has just been given the thing he believes he will never possess.

Tranqil Ease

After World War II, during the decades that he worked in the family furniture store, my father's talent for engineering and invention lay fallow, save for the odd gadget—the magnetic toothbrush!—that never left our home, and the occasional repair, such as the vacuum cleaner motor installed in the ancient organ caked in dust in the basement, which allowed us to play it (badly) and which, we later learned, meant that it was no longer worth the fortune it would have been worth untinkered with.

Then came the 1970s. My father, unimpressed with the vibrating chairs that had come to popularity, developed a motor that, when installed in furniture, created an interference wave pattern. This effect was closer to that of being massaged by two hands than to being mechanically goosed. Within a few years he had patented the Tranqil Ease (intentionally misspelled, as was the fad at the time) and was selling components to major purveyors of chairs, including Sears. He later expanded the business to include wands that slipped under the mattress. (A disastrous collaboration with a waterbed company in San Francisco—the result of his capacity to see only the best in people—nearly bankrupted him at one point. He kept his round waterbed, however, for the rest of his life.)

Meanwhile, the big chains were steadily encroaching on the furniture business, and the family stores, in two locations, faltered. My grandfather had started the business in the 1930s, after years of working at Sears and an almost equal number of years of urging from my grandmother. The original store was a child's paradise, spread over three levels, with a deserted cashier's booth like a ghost motel suspended above the main floor. (Years earlier, bills of sale had been written up by the men—and they were all men—on the floor, then clipped to a pulley and yanked heavenward to the cashier.) The basement had a trapdoor entrance via the sidewalk and a big coal-burning furnace. On the top floor, often deserted, were Philco appliances and dinette sets with plastic bowls of plastic fruit. My sister and I would spend hours up there playing house. In the 1960s, my father and uncle each opened their own enormous exurban branch with cost-effective floor space, devoid of quaint contraptions. The original store, in what became a violent neighborhood, was finally closed after my grandfather was robbed at gunpoint and locked in the bathroom. From then on, he spent his days at my uncle's store, mostly sitting at a desk by the clerical pool, deep into his nineties.

By the late 1970s, it was impossible to compete with Levitz and its like; the store was converted into a cash-and-carry, as-is, no-frills show room with deep discounts on factory overruns and discontinued styles. This was a temporary goldmine—even I, a high school kid, was allowed on the sales floor because there weren't enough people to write up orders fast enough. My father, who'd never spent much on himself, was seen driving around town in what the cousins referred to as the pimp mobile; he also bought an airplane. Then it went bust. (If imitation is the sincerest form of flattery, then the business's bigger corporate admirers flattered it to death.)

By that time, the Tranqil Ease patent was bringing in enough money that my father opened a factory to manufacture the components himself. He was convinced, perhaps correctly, that when used in chairs and mattresses the motors triggered alpha waves. He advertised heavily and sold a lot of units.

When Brendan was a baby he sent us a Tranqil Ease rod for the crib. We hoped it might encourage our never-sleeping baby to sleep. Instead, the baby puked. After my father's death, my stepmother ran the factory for awhile, then sold it to someone else. Recently, I found the rod from under Brendan's crib. The baby is almost college-age and plans to major in physics.

Prize Dogs

Sean has developed an aptitude for acquiring small stuffed dogs—none as big as Rascal—at arcades. His hand, as he maneuvers the metal cranes and pincers—designed to grip your desired plush-toy, then lose it in the final seconds before it reaches the prize chute—is quite unerring. Again and again, he beats the odds and wins. Those pups are all over the house.

The Thing with Wings

I have two of my sister's paintings on my walls—
one a beachscape that was a wedding gift and the
other an enormous vermillion flower that she
gave me on my fortieth birthday. I have a clay
pitcher she made, that sits next to the luminous
vase from my grandfather. I have the usual gifts
an older sister gives a younger over the years—
bracelets, earrings, blouses. And then there is a
ridiculous stuffed creature that sits on the arm
of the chair that I read in; she gave it to me one
year on my birthday when, she said, she had run
out of ideas. I think it's supposed to be some sort
of bear, although it has gossamer wings sewn on.
It's neither cute nor pretty. It stays on my chair
because it is an impossible life form, a fiction, like
our childhood, as my sister and I remember it.

My Grandmother Bern's Recipes

They take forever to make. I am lazy. They are bad for you—high calorie, low fiber, high cholesterol and fat—not to mention Crisco. They wouldn't taste the same, I am convinced, if I made them. The cakes would fail to rise. That's not why I don't bake them. I can't bear to open that stained scotch plaid box of index cards on which my mother's handwriting—loopy and blue—is fading fast.

The Lamps

Although my maternal great aunt B lived into her nineties, she had no idea who anybody was in her final years. (The last time I phoned her, I kept saying, "This is Dawn," and she kept saying, "I don't have a dog! Stop calling me!") She had been an artist and had worked for years at Chicago's Art Institute. At 80 she'd been shockingly beautiful, with the kind of radiance some old women have. In the end, insensate, she was very close to blind and deaf; not only did she not know who I was when I visited, I'm not convinced she knew someone was there.

"If I get like that," my mother said repeatedly, "just shove a pillow over my face." I believe she meant it. She was obsessed with the manner in which she would die, starting around the time she was 60. ("Just remember," she'd say, "your father died with his shoes on." And, "When I go, I'm going fast, so don't be surprised.")

When B at last expired in Chicago, my mother first protested my coming to the funeral (expensive, etc.) and then insisted on picking me up at the airport when I called to say I was on my way. Stepping into the backseat of the big sedan my stepfather drove, I was keenly aware that the days when they would pick me up at an airport were sharply numbered.

My mother had a particular idea about glamour, most of it involving Chicago's Michigan Avenue —she never quite recovered from moving to Milwaukee when, at 20, she married my father. Chicago for her was the emerald city. Any time we needed a dress for an occasion, or simply needed an occasion to spend money, we would drive in, or take the Milwaukee Road train to Union Station, go to Saks, then walk the Miracle Mile.

The night before B's funeral we went to dinner at the Ritz. (My mother liked the coffee shop, which had a better vantage than the dining room for people watching; in truth, she was indifferent to food but craved atmosphere. In the years between her divorce and remarriage, she led art tours from Milwaukee to Chicago, always ending at the Ritz. She married my stepfather there, in a professional discount deal.) After dinner we headed over to the twelfth-floor lobby of the Four Seasons to listen to someone play on the piano the kind of music that, if you are my age, you associate with your parents.

After the funeral, with hours to kill before they drove me to the airport, my mother and stepfather went to visit a few of the girls, now nearing 80, with whom my mother had gone to grammar school. This seemed liked a good time for me to take a walk to the nearby mall, where I spotted the ideal lamps for my living room. Instead of buying them and having them shipped, which would have made sense, I decided to go to the New York branch of the store and haul them home—roughly half my weight in lamps—on the PATH train to New Jersey. ("Is there some reason," my mother said to me countless times, "why you feel the need to do everything the hard way?")

That was my final trip with my mother to Chicago; she was dead within the year. My stepfather most likely was already harboring the cancer that would kill him. The lights shine in my living room.

The View

E and I met at 23 through a mutual friend. Two years later we sealed our friendship over a long brunch during which we masticated a mutual ex- boyfriend, to whom each of us had been introduced in turn by our mutual now-ex-friend. E was an artist and graphic designer living in a studio in the West Village. She was also a black belt in karate, a world-class listener, and a scary-smart cookie. We used to meet at our favorite dive on Christopher Street until, during the worst of the city's AIDS epidemic, it, along with many other West Village businesses, was ominously shuttered. Our friendship turned nomadic. E moved to a bigger place in Chelsea with huge east-facing windows; every Sunday she would walk down to Jane Street and buzz me. We would walk for miles, sometimes in the freezing cold, with no real destination. She might point out a visual grace note of the city that I'd never noticed, or stop and admire a fabric in a window. If she bought a sheet or a drape, she was acutely aware of the slightest gradation of color. Her own work, though, was black and white. She drew meticulously detailed landscapes and cityscapes—she made you understand a building's soul.

Our Sunday walks ended when E's mother was dying and she went upstate on weekends; before long, I left the city and had a child, then two. Still, we saw each other for great gulps of conversation—or as often as we could, given that she worked 60-70 hour weeks at a job she wanted to leave. No good deed goes unpunished: I introduced her to the career Jedi who was a contributing editor at the magazine where I worked, and she helped E find an ideal situation—in Boston.

Like everyone who leaves New York, E planned to come back often…and didn't. I'm not great at the five-hour trek myself, and anyone will tell you I'm awful on the phone. (When I was single I rarely bothered to answer, letting it ring and ring, or, after my father bought me a machine in an act of enlightened self-interest, letting the messages pile up.) But in person we like nothing better, still, than the miles-long conversation that could take us anywhere. Walking down a sidewalk or through a park, she sees details that I miss, in nature, in design, and in my life. She sees me—and I, her—in split-screen, in middle-age (operating under the presumption that we will be hitting the century mark) and at 23. Because she is my friend, and kind, she sees me, perhaps, as I never was but wanted to be. She may see my future more clearly than I do. I like to imagine the two of us wandering into our seventies, if we are lucky, maybe catching an early bird special and a cappuccino after a brisk walk. On my wall I have the view in black and white, as she drew it, of the rooftops slanting this way and that, seen through her studio window in the Village.

Peacock Feathers

I asked my kids if there was anything in particular that they wanted from my mother's house and they both chimed in: "The peacock feathers!"

"What peacock feathers?" I said.

"Right when you walk in the living room," Sean said.

"How could you miss that, Mom?" said Brendan.

But miss them I did. What I remembered about my mother's living room was the heavy glass coffee table, shaped like a flat-topped tunnel, that every child who entered the house delighted in crawling through—until Sean, at two, on hands and knees, by imperceptible fluke shift, caused it to shatter in huge, heavy shards. Amazingly, he emerged without a scratch, frightened only by all the commotion as we picked up hunks of glass that could have cut a jugular, and pulled shard after shard from the thick white carpet. The table was replaced by one in Plexiglas. I remembered, too, the wood-carved statue of the woman who was me as a pre-teenager, and the Saturday hours that I posed in a swimsuit for my mother in her empty classroom at the university, and how, afterward,

we'd go out for chili dogs, and how sometimes my
mother relaxed and laughed deeply. I remembered
the white leather sofa where she'd hold her baby
grandsons and where, sometimes late at night, after
my stepfather was asleep, we would sit and eat vanilla
ice cream drowning in cognac—and how, once in
a very great while, she'd tell me a story I'd never
heard before: How an aunt, for instance, a woman
long dead by the time I was born, had shared my
mother's bedroom after her only child had died.
("She cried herself to sleep every night in the bed
next to mine," my mother said.) I remembered the
Oriental desk, crammed with papers and notes
meant for me to discover after my mother's death,
and the magenta batik that my mother had made
and hung on the wall, and a triptych, in more of my
mother's colors—corals, pinks, reds—occupying
the space above the fireplace that she always wanted
to fix in some way that I can't recall.

When I got to my mother's house, I immediately
saw what my children requested: a bouquet of
peacock feathers in a gold vase on the floor—
eye-high to a toddler, a thing that a child might
well remember best, much as I remembered my
Grandmother Raffel's china cat. And so the vase
came home, not much worse for travel, the tips of
the feathers blue and brilliant green, like seven eyes.

My Father's Hat

When I picture my father, I picture him wearing a hat. Not a business hat—I don't believe I ever saw him wearing one of those—but the goofy floppy cotton hats he wore in the sun and the fuzzy faux bombers he wore when he flew or when the weather was cold, as it so often was. (There was also a knitted "Albert" hat left over from the 1970s—Albert being the weather-cat mascot of the local TV station where my father taped commercials for the furniture store. The hat was black and white with a cat's face made with googly-eyes, a red nose pompon, and whiskers, and with the name Albert written on the brim. I eventually gave it to an art director friend named Albert, who properly appreciated it.) The foremost image I have of my father is of him standing on the wing of his Cessna with a certain suede hat on his head, getting ready for takeoff, a memory that, I'm sure, has been reinforced because I have a photograph of it. Brendan, as a baby, found this hat hilarious; it triggered propulsive glee.

It's sitting in a bin in my closet. No one wears it.

The Photograph That Proves That My Memories Were Wrong

I have hundreds of photographs taken before the art of the image went digital. Some I snapped myself; others were given to me or inherited. Some are dated; many are not. Although I have discarded the ones that I had no idea who the subjects were, I have many more of people who might be, say, Great Uncle Jack and Great Uncle Max—but I don't know which is which, and there is no one left to ask. I have far too many pictures of my children, some of them duplicates. Some are in albums, many are not. Some are stuck together from humidity, neglect. I did my best to separate the photos that rightly belonged to my stepsiblings from the ones I meant to keep, but the task was confusing, the lines of family blurred. In the oldest of the images, my stepfather was revealed to me, posthumously, young. My mother's teenage good looks shocked us all, all over again.

The photo that undid me, though, was one taken of me. Among my clearest memories is that of wrapping a gift to look like a castle, complete with cutout parapets. I remember building the thing in my father's house, on break from my freshman year in college, cutting and taping in his living room. But in my mother's drawers I found a picture of myself holding that gift-wrapped castle in the house I grew up in, not my father's lake house, and by the photo's date, still at home in high school. The photo made me ill. I thought I might vomit. There was no possibility that there had been two such gift-wrapped packages at different times and places. My memory, a thing I'd have sworn to, was incontrovertibly wrong. What else have I misremembered? What pieces of my past are so ungraspable they've shifted shape and form?

The Thing I Never Found

If memory serves me, my Grandma and Grandpa Bern once booked an hour in a do-it-yourself recording studio, and cut a 45 of themselves singing together in Hungarian. I looked through every dusty box, every stack of LPs and 45s in my mother's house; it wasn't there. Nowadays, people make videotapes, elaborate ones. But that one slim disk was the last place on earth where my grandparent's voices were trapped in song.

The Ruby Watch

I used to see it only when my mother took me
to look in the safety deposit box she kept in the
vault at the bank. It is a small copper watch set
with rubies that her father bought for her when
she graduated from high school. My mother never
wore it—at least, not during the years I knew her
as my mother. It wasn't her style and it was small
for her wrist. I have always loved that watch. Not
long before my mother died she gave it to me,
surprised that I wanted such a thing. Despite
repairs, its hands move sporadically and it requires
winding. Still, I sometimes clasp it on my wrist.
It's yet another watch in the family that marks the
hours' passage in its own sweet time.

The Record Album

My senior year in college the woman in the next dorm room, who was a hallway acquaintance, was giving all of her record albums away. She insisted she didn't want them. After several rounds of "Are you sure?" I accepted Otis Redding. The next week, I heard she had tried to commit suicide and had been taken home. For the rest of the time I was there, she didn't return and I never saw or heard from her again. For months I was haunted by the fact that I'd had no clue what was going on in her life, inside her head, on the other side of a thin wall; in fact, I had taken personally her recent aloofness (the album giveaway notwithstanding) and had wondered what I might have done to offend her. This was not my first experience with someone suicidal. In an effort to better understand, I had taken 20 hours of crisis intervention training during my freshman year, qualifying to work on a soon-to-open suicide hotline. (It never took off—we volunteers mostly sat for hours in a cold church basement waiting for the phone to ring.) But by my senior year, my own drama was playing so loudly in my head that I utterly failed to hear that of the woman next door.

I keep that album pressed between the Leo
Kotke and Stevie Wonder and John Prine and
Beatles and Paul Simon albums I collected in the
1970s. I never hear "Sittin' on the Dock of the
Bay" without feeling a certain nostalgia for a place
I have never been, and without thinking of that
woman, whose last name I cannot recall.

Yosemite And The Range Of Light

Where the poster came from I don't know. It's a framed Ansel Adams print, an image you might find in any dorm room. Because we moved into our house the same week Brendan was born (our closing was delayed by a month and the baby came early), the household was haphazard. Boxes sat unopened, rooms went unpainted, and items of uncertain origin appeared on walls and shelves. The poster hung in the sitting room outside our bedroom where I used to nurse the babies in a second-hand chair in the middle of the night. I was unwilling to use the popular Ferber method, in which you let the baby cry for set increments of time until he learns to sleep through the night. Self-comfort was the concept. I couldn't wait it out, couldn't comfort myself while the baby was crying. And so I was up at two and four and six a.m. and off to work in the morning, bleary-eyed, hormonal, night and day. Sometimes I sat with the lights off but more often they were on, set dim, and I was looking at that picture, made impressionistic by myopia and extreme astigmatism. With every waking and would-be sleeping moment spoken for, and with my body (though no longer harboring a fetal secret sharer) not my own, that poster opened up a cold bright world of possibility. I sang in the night to my sons in that chair. I dreamed while awake, began a novel in my head. That was a world—a universe, not just a room—of my own where, as my sons took what they needed from my body—their weight in my arms, their heat on my chest—I made all the rules.

Now I sleep through the night. The novel, committed to paper, then printed and bound, stitched up, became a fact, never again to have the potency it had when it resided in my head. It is finite now, its possibilities contained. Brendan is bigger than I am, and Sean will soon be too. But I can still feel in me that great range of light—the call of the world, the child's insistent suckle.

The Glass Angel

I became intrigued with angels when I was assigned to write an article about them in 1990. A spate of angel books was published that year, as the quick trip *du jour* to salvation. I ended up probing the subject more deeply than my editors required or desired, starting with the Bible, on through the Middle Ages and into the Twentieth Century, and was surprised to learn how many people, secretly or otherwise, believed. (My husband felt the difference between Protestantism and Catholicism was encapsulated by a juxtaposition of quotes in which a minister pronounced angels a beautiful metaphor and a priest proclaimed them real.) I spoke with self-styled "angelologists" who sounded as if something were fluttering in their heads, and with thinkers who could not be taken lightly. The article, when it was published, had one of the highest readerships of anything in the magazine that year.

Three years later when Brendan was born, my mother-in-law bought an angel plate to hang over his crib in what struck us all as a perfect interfaith emblem of faith.

I didn't think much more about angels until, shortly after my father's death in December 2000, on a day when the wind caused the windows in the office where I worked to rattle menacingly, I bought one made of glass. It broke. I still have the pieces.

The Angel From Russia

When I found out that my friend T had taught at a study-abroad writer's workshop in St. Petersburg, Russia—a city I had wanted to visit ever since I read *War and Peace* for the first time at 13—I asked her for the name of the person running the program and threw myself at his feet. In the summer of 2007 I got my chance to teach short story writing to American and Canadian students in that fiercely gorgeous city, named and unnamed and renamed for a Tsar—and for the keeper of heaven.

I spoke enough Russian to think I could find my way around alone. The first time I left my hotel, though, I got utterly lost. (One man gave me directions into what turned out to be a dark, gated enclosure, causing me to wonder whether this was where I would die. It turned out to be nothing more insidious than the entrance to the wrong hotel.) As it happened, I had repeatedly walked past the correct hotel because, in my jetlagged state, I hadn't registered that it bore no sign in any language that said "hotel," only one that said, inexplicably (in English), "Pepsi." Nevertheless, the only time I was in real danger was when I made the not-very-smart decision to cut through an alley (and over the bridge with the golden griffins) to the nearest fake Starbucks at seven a.m., an hour at which, during the White Nights, most people are asleep and the streets are deserted. As if out of nowhere, a group of belligerent looking young women blocked me in the alleyway, and appeared ready, I feared, to pummel me, or worse. I was just about to throw my coffee at them and run, when one of them asked, in Russian, whether I was French. Stunned, I answered in English that I was American. At that, they let me go. (I have no idea what they had against the French; I'd have thought it would be far more perilous to be American. For some reason, perhaps because I was walking around in a raincoat I had bought in Paris, the Russians repeatedly mistook me for French—something no actual French person has ever done.)

On returning home I sent an email to a young woman with whom I had worked at a magazine in Manhattan and who was by then living in Burundi:

> One of our guides told us we were literally standing on bones, as so many serfs died building this city that sprang from Peter the Great's imagination. History seems to seep out of the pores of its grand buildings. We were made to feel the ghosts of those disappeared

to the gulag and of the millions who starved to death during the siege of Leningrad (it was said that anyone with color in his cheeks was known to have been eating human flesh, the sole remaining source of protein). Today you see almost Soviet-style grocery stores—cheap, crummy produce; cramped, dirty aisles—just blocks from designer clothing emporiums with prices double what you'd find in New York. New restaurants and fake Starbucks (familiar round logo; a name that is a transliteration of "coffee house") are everywhere, but you can count on them being out of half of what's on the menu, or out of cups, or out of coffee... and it takes forever to get anything, if, in fact, what you ordered ever arrives. On a daily basis, the bus does not come, the laundry is closed because the laundry lady is at the dacha, and there is no hot water. But how can you not love a city with 24-hour bookstores (ask any Russian and he or she can recite Mayakovsky and Dostoevsky by heart) and where the light is spectacular for 20 hours of the day. On the summer solstice people dance wildly along the riverbanks and cram onto boats, clogging the Neva, blasting American techno pop and drinking quarts of vodka...

One morning I walked into the Kazanskaya Cathedral, where the great General Kutuzov, hero of the Napoleanic war, is buried. During the Soviet years it became a museum of the history of religion, or, as many Russians referred to it, a history of atheism. Now it is again a magnificent church. (One Russian woman told us that restoring the city's imperial place names "keeps us from feeling total despair.")

I bought the angel there in the cathedral. It is the size, perhaps, of a strawberry from an American grocery store. I keep it in my purse.

The Plate I Thought I'd Lost That My Mother Had All Along

The trip to Greece was an accident, a mishap, the result of a miscommunication that would not have occurred in the age of email. It was the end of 1977; I was going to visit my friend C in London and she wrote asking whether I would like to take a brief side trip, say, to Scotland. I wrote back and said yes. When I arrived in London, C told me she had found a deal on sunny Athens and since there had been no time to write back and forth, she had already purchased our nonrefundable airline tickets.

Athens was not sunny, not in terms of weather or general atmosphere—it was a military dictatorship—and not in terms of my mood either. We were broke and I can't say that I was a very good sport. We froze in a rented room we'd found late at night, having landed in Athens with no plan of action, then moved to a YMCA where we shared a not-much-warmer room with eight other women and one sorry toilet. The ruins, distracted as we were, were hard to comprehend. What food we could afford was cheap and greasy or gristled. Delphi, arrived at by rickety bus, was

gorgeous—I remember sitting on the crest of a hill overlooking a sweeping expanse of greenery, eating goat's milk yogurt on a cloudless day—but mostly we were hungry and cold. (The fault lay not in the least with Greece or its citizens. One day we were invited off the street into an elderly woman's home for cookies, and another day into a church to view the end of a wedding. I shudder to think what would have happened if we had approached New York in a similar manner.) Back in Athens for New Year's Eve we tried to extend a coffee in a café until midnight but found ourselves back on the street with more than an hour to go. Everywhere we went, we were accosted by men who assumed two women alone were whores, or at the least, fair game.

I bought one thing in Greece: a cloisonné plate—my mother had taught me to appreciate that art, in which luminous fragments redound to a whole—in red and green and gold, in rings of starburst. What I paid I can't recall, although I do remember standing in the store and thinking that the plate was remarkably inexpensive, and worth skipping a meal. I took a redeye back to London (C stayed in Greece), then stood outdoors in sub-freezing weather for more than four hours waiting to get a seat home on Laker Airlines that, in turn, was seven hours late to JFK. By the time

I got back to college in Rhode Island, I was on the brink of being sicker than I'd ever been in my life, or have been since—shaking with fever, irrational, unable to manage food for days. (C, I later learned, was equally sick in the Y in Greece). I ended a relationship precipitously out of utter confusion and stayed in my room. I had brought home a handful of snapshots, many blurred, a teacup from London, a cloisonné plate. I vaguely remember somebody using the latter, much to my dismay, as an ashtray.

Thirty years later I found in a box marked "Dawn" in my mother's basement—along with my plastic-bound thesis, my yearbook, a pile of spiral notebooks, and my bachelor's degree—that shining plate. These artifacts are of a time that in many ways I would rather forget—a piece of my life that was not of a piece with the rest. Between 20 and 22, I was too often carelessly unkind, and also often despairing. That I belonged nowhere, geographically or emotionally, makes those years hard to light, even in the flattering incandescence of memory.

And yet I am glad that my mother saved that vision in fragments. It belongs to me.

What My Mother Thought She Had Lost That I Found

1. A lot of her jewelry. She'd called me, tremendously upset, believing that it had been stolen. I found it in a white trash bag in the back of the closet, hidden, I suspect, out of fear of theft. I also found the earrings that go with the crystal necklace that I wear all the time.

2. The deeds to the gravesites. They were in the attic.

144   Dawn Raffel

The Daughter Vase

There were two matching vases in my mother's downstairs bathroom—a big one and a little one. I took the little one and left the big one in the house for the resellers to sell. Why did I do that?

Uncle Irving's Devil

He was my Grandfather Bern's brother, one of the younger siblings who was brought over with his parents from Kisvárda, Hungary by—depending on who you believed—either my grandfather or his older sister. Another brother had died in the great influenza epidemic that had swept through Europe in the second decade of the Twentieth Century; others had not survived childhood. Irving made a fortune and died in middle age, of a heart attack over dinner in a restaurant with his wife, my great aunt L.

I met him only twice. The first time, I was four. He gave me a red china devil with a pipe cleaner tail and a fireman's hat slung on a chain around its neck. When I was nine he gave me a bag of cosmetics (beauty being one of his businesses). When I was eleven years old, he died; I was inconsolable. (Great Aunt L, who went on to be widowed again, was diagnosed with depression; by the time someone figured out that her fatigue and pain were, in fact, caused by cancer, it had already metastasized.)

My mother kept up with his children—her

cousins—for a while, and then that branch of the family simply dropped off like a piece of a continent into a sea.

My grandparents' generation—often short of space and short of temper; they fought robustly—would cram around metal folding tables, finding occasions to meet. Their descendants moved on, all over the country; we, as we say, "lost touch." In this, our family is by no means unique; witness the popularity of reunion websites. But what one finds online—the satisfaction of scratching a certain curious itch—doesn't salve a thirty- or forty-year lapse.

For all that my mother accrued in material possessions, her most prized collection was of people—of cousins, of "once-removeds," of friends. She had dozens of genuine friendships—not acquaintanceships—that lasted for decades. These were not colleagues; no one was networking. No one had girls' getaways, pre-packaged. Instead, they had the phone—rotary, princess, cordless, cell. They had the car for the afternoon. These relationships were messy and complicated. Many of the women—all "Mrs." to me, until I went to college—are dead now. Their kids, who once piled with me into backseats of cars, are all over the country, all over the world, as are the snapped-off branches of my family.

I have a little devil.

Medals

We bought our house from a man who'd been living there with both his lover and his mother. When his mother died he was getting ready to fix up the place to put it on the market; we offered to buy it as-is. This meant that nothing had been repaired or repainted (the ghost of a Dustbuster past haunted the kitchen wall; he had apparently painted around the device). Various items remained in the house. Some, such as the old stuffed chair in the sitting room where I sat and nursed my babies in the night, were deliberate leave-behinds, furnishings he told us he no longer needed. Others took a while to find, including the silver medals of saints stuck in odd spots on the walls.

Both of the apartments where I had lived with my husband in Manhattan had been refurbished and delivered as if new. But in our house, it is impossible not to notice that other lives have been lived within its walls. The previous owner's mother, for all we know, died here; if not, then she was certainly dying, surrounded by emblems of faith.

The house has been expanded—to the back

and to the side and now up. But its core is more than 100 years old. Its walls have yielded layers and layers of paint. We found floors under floors.

Some people believe that the souls of the dead hover near the house that is the body, until the body's burial. What about the house of that house? The bodies have certainly left their marks—made scratches and dents, left scuffs and prints. And what of the disturbance that is breath?

.

The Mirror

The man who sold the house to us also left the mirror in the upstairs bathroom, gilt-framed, hanging from two big nails. Its surface has reflected not only his face and that of his lover and of his mother, but also my face and my husband's as we've aged, and those of the children as they've grown. A different set of faces every day—the work of gravity on mine, the efflorescence of the children's; steam.

Garnet Earrings

Right around the time I was 30, I was having a great deal of difficulty selling the stories I was writing. It seemed endlessly my fate that in any competition I would be among the finalists but never the winner, or that I would receive a letter from an editor of a literary journal stating something to the effect that she'd had to choose between my story and another, and in the end, well.....

I had meanwhile gotten it into my head that I wanted a pair of red earrings—ruby, garnet; didn't matter—and that I would buy them for myself as a reward, as soon as I made a sale. Months went by. More rejections. More months. One day I was walking on 47th Street, New York's diamond row, when, in the window of a resale store, I saw the exact earrings I wanted—garnet drops with diamond chips, set in gold, old. They were one-of-a-kind and I knew they'd be gone in a week, if not sooner. They cost $115, which was beyond my budget, and which, contrary to character, I paid on the spot.

A few weeks later I sold a story; within the next year, seven more. For awhile, I attributed this to the purchase of the earrings, an advance on success, so much so that my friend E paid $100 for a bracelet she could also not afford and waited for the luck to pour in. It didn't quite work according to plan, but the premise—to act as if you're already in the place you'd like to be—is not entirely unsound.

I wear the earrings often. They belonged to a woman I know nothing about. I have sometimes wondered whether her features and her coloring were anything like mine, and how she dressed, how old she was and who she loved, and whether she thought she was lucky.

The Dictionary

Before I started college, my mother and I drove into Chicago to shop. We stopped at Brentano's now defunct bookstore, and there my mother bought me a hardbound copy of *Webster's Second College Edition New World Dictionary of the American Language,* a heavy brown volume with extra-thin pages and old-fashioned finger tabs for each letter.

The letters on the finger tabs have mostly worn off and the gold-embossed cover is splitting from the spine. The contents need revision: Names of many countries have become obsolete, and absent are words such as *Internet, cyberspace,* and *globalization.*

My children have no patience for a printed dictionary. Their laptops—another word not present in *Webster's Second College Edition*—weigh less than 1692 pages of paper.

My dictionary sits on my desk, a relic of a world from which everyone roughly my age lives in exile. Opening it, I am standing once more on the cusp of my life, with my beautiful mother, unburdened of years. My dictionary holds between its covers all the words we might have said.

Acknowledgements

For their unwavering support, I would like to thank Melanie Jackson, Debra Di Blasi, Noreen Tomassi, Terese Svoboda, and always my husband, Michael Evers. A deep debt of gratitude is owed to my family. Thanks are also due to Caitlin McKenna, Patricia Volk, and the editors of the magazines who first published these chapters: Samuel Ligon, Donald Breckenridge, Tim Small, Carroll Beauvais, Mikael Awake, David McLendon, J.D. Scott, Luke Goebel, Matt Bell, Scott Garson, Ronnie Scott, and Douglas Glover. Finally, a special thank you to Joyce Raffel for persuading me to take home the mug.

About The Author

Dawn Raffel is the author of two story collections, *Further Adventures in the Restless Universe* and *In the Year of Long Division*, and a novel, *Carrying the Body*. Her fiction has appeared in *O, The Oprah Magazine, BOMB, Conjunctions, The Anchor Book of New American Short Stories, The Quarterly, NOON,* and many others. She has taught in the MFA program at Columbia University, and at Summer Literary Seminars in Montreal, Canada, and St. Petersburg, Russia. She is an editor at large for *Reader's Digest* and the editor of *The Literarian,* the online journal for the Center for Fiction in New York City.